OCTOPUSES

by Emma Bassier

Cody Koala
An Imprint of Pop!
popbooksonline.com

abdobooks.com
Published by Pop!, a division of ABDO, PO Box 398166, Minneapolis, Minnesota 55439. Copyright © 2020 by POP, LLC. International copyrights reserved in all countries. No part of this book may be reproduced in any form without written permission from the publisher. Pop!™ is a trademark and logo of POP, LLC.

Printed in the United States of America, North Mankato, Minnesota
052019
092019
THIS BOOK CONTAINS RECYCLED MATERIALS

Cover Photo: iStockphoto
Interior Photos: iStockphoto, 1, 5 (top), 5 (bottom left), 5 (bottom right), 7, 9, 11, 15; Jeff Rotman/Science Source, 12–13; Shutterstock Images, 14; Victor Habbick Visions/Science Source, 17; Jeff Rotman/Science Source, 19; Danté Fenolio/Science Source, 20

Editor: Meg Gaertner
Series Designer: Sophie Geister-Jones

Library of Congress Control Number: 2018964499
Publisher's Cataloging-in-Publication Data
Names: Bassier, Emma, author.
Title: Octopuses / by Emma Bassier.
Description: Minneapolis, Minnesota : Pop!, 2020 | Series: Ocean animals | Includes online resources and index.
Identifiers: ISBN 9781532163401 (lib. bdg.) | ISBN 9781644940136 (pbk.) | ISBN 9781532164842 (ebook)
Subjects: LCSH: Octopuses--Juvenile literature. | Invertebrates--Behavior--Juvenile literature. | Octopi--Juvenile literature. | Ocean animals--Juvenile literature.
Classification: DDC 594.56--dc23

Hello! My name is
Cody Koala

Pop open this book and you'll find QR codes like this one, loaded with information, so you can learn even more!

Scan this code* and others like it while you read, or visit the website below to make this book pop.

popbooksonline.com/octopuses

*Scanning QR codes requires a web-enabled smart device with a QR code reader app and a camera.

Table of Contents

Chapter 1
Soft Bodies 4

Chapter 2
Movement 8

Chapter 3
Smart Defense 10

Chapter 4
Life Cycle 18

Making Connections 22
Glossary 23
Index 24
Online Resources 24

Chapter 1

Soft Bodies

Octopuses are soft-bodied ocean animals. They live alone on the ocean floor.

Watch a video here!

An octopus has a large **mantle**. Eight arms extend from the mantle. Each arm is covered with **suckers**. An octopus uses its suckers to grab objects or food.

> Octopuses have blue blood and three hearts.

Chapter 2

Movement

Octopuses use their arms to walk along the ocean floor. They also move by pushing water out of their **mantles**. The water shoots back and pushes the octopus forward.

Learn more here!

Chapter 3

Smart Defense

Many animals eat octopuses. But octopuses are good at escaping from **predators**. They use **camouflage** to hide. They blend in with their environments.

Octopuses can also shoot out dark ink. The ink hurts the predator's sense of taste or smell.

The ink also hurts the predator's eyes. It surprises the predator. The octopus has time to escape.

Octopuses do not have bones. This allows them to fit into very tight places.

An octopus might hide inside a shell.

Octopuses can regrow arms they have lost.

Octopuses are **carnivores**. They eat all kinds of ocean animals. An octopus has a sharp beak inside its **mantle**. It chops food into small pieces to eat.

Chapter 4

Life Cycle

A **female** octopus lays eggs only once during her life. She lays eggs in the water. Then she stays with the eggs to keep them safe.

eggs

Complete an activity here!

The eggs hatch after a few months. The mother dies soon after. The baby octopuses can already live on their own. Most octopuses live for one to two years.

Making Connections

Text-to-Self

Octopuses are carnivores. They eat meat. What foods do you like to eat?

Text-to-Text

Have you read other books about animals that do not have bones? How are those animals similar to or different from octopuses?

Text-to-World

Octopuses can use camouflage to hide from predators. What other animals use camouflage?

Glossary

camouflage – the ability to hide by blending in with the environment.

carnivore – an animal that eats only meat.

female – a person or animal of the sex that can have babies or lay eggs.

mantle – the head of an octopus.

predator – an animal that hunts other animals.

sucker – a small circle on an octopus arm that helps it attach to something and grip tightly.

Index

arms, 6, 7, 8, 15

beak, 16, 17

camouflage, 10

eggs, 18, 19, 21

food, 6, 16

ink, 12–13

mantles, 6, 7, 8, 16

suckers, 6, 7

Online Resources

popbooksonline.com

Thanks for reading this Cody Koala book!

Scan this code* and others like it in this book, or visit the website below to make this book pop!

popbooksonline.com/octopuses

*Scanning QR codes requires a web-enabled smart device with a QR code reader app and a camera.